THROUGH THE FIRE

A SURVIVOR'S STORY

By

Jaye Ebony

Acknowledgment

My families, both near and far, I love you all and thank you for always believing in me! This is for anyone who picked up my book. I hope and pray by me, telling my truths that it may seem easier to give up but if you throw in the towel too soon, you will never reach or see the finish line! You will never see the purpose for your life. I endured it, I lived it, and I survived it!

Emily B- I love you, my sister from another. Blood could not make us any closer- I love you to the moon and back!

DEDICATION

To my Son, My Lil Big Man,

You're my heart and soul. I love you; you're my reason for breathing.

The impact you have had on my life is more than you will ever know.

You were and still are, my motivation to make you proud. I love you!

CONTENTS

Acknowledgment   iii

Dedication   iv

Foreword   1

Introduction   2

Part 1   6

Chapter 1   7

Chapter 2   14

Chapter 3   17

Chapter 4   20

Part 2   25

Chapter 1   26

Chapter 2   28

Chapter 3   30

Chapter 5   34

Part 3   35

Chapter 1   36

Chapter 2   40

Chapter 3   43

Chapter 4   49

Chapter 5   51

Chapter 6   54

Chapter 7   56

Chapter 8   59

Chapter 9   62

Chapter 10   65

Chapter 11   68

Chapter 12   73

Chapter 13   77

Chapter 14   79

Chapter 15   82

Chapter 16   84

Chapter 17   87

Chapter 18   91

Chapter 19   94

Chapter 20   98

Domestic Violence Facts   107

FOREWORD

This book is a story of a true survivor.

Since the beginning, I have watched her story unfold in ways I never imagined possible, when we first met.

Before my eyes, she has transformed from once being lost, broken and scared, to becoming strong, independent, and triumphant.

To be where she is today, after all the obstacles she has been through, is truly a miracle. And it has been my pleasure to witness this miracle unfold.

This book gives her the opportunity to share her story with the world in her own words.

Carla T.

Introduction

Love is stronger than any addiction, and that is a hard lesson that I have learned. In this book, I not only want to share my story, but I also want to tell my story. I wanted to tell my truth because I have lived a life full of many struggles and obstacles. At times, it seemed easier to give up or give in, but I have learned that no matter what and how life may present itself, you DO NOT just give up or give in because you will never see the provisions that the "Almighty" has for your life. (I understand that people may have different views on religion, but I am just speaking for myself and what God has done in my life personally.) I chose to expose my life because I have experienced it, I have lived it, and I survived it! All the trials and tribulations that my life has given me, have made me a stronger individual. I have learned a lot about myself, and I am continuing to learn more and more every day about myself. I have learned that I am very strong and determined. I hope that telling my story and my truth will resonate and help someone in need. My memory may not be 100%, but these are the stories in the deep memory that I recall in my life. They have been verified memories by my sister, who was also there for the memories and moments.

Intro-

"How did I get here?" There I was, holding on for dear life. I was never afraid of heights, but in this particular case, I was terrified it was a 50/50 chance that I could have taken the express route down, all depending on one man's emotion. I sat there dangling out the window from the 4th floor of my apartment window. Half of my body was cut off by the window as I hung on for dear life by the mercy of my captor. My bed was in the corner next to the window. I could not believe I was dangling out of the window while he continued to lay his hands on the bottom half of my body, which was not hanging out the window. I was lying on my back and waist down. I was on my bed, but one forceful push was all it would have taken for me to have met my maker. We were in a fight; well, correction, it was not considered a technical fight because I knew better than to fight back. I was not a fighter and I was not equipped for the pain and torture that I subjected my body to. My body had grown numb to the pain, but my heart was very invested.

I did not see an easy way out unscathed through it all, no matter what, but for some reason, I loved him through it all. It was yet another fight, but this one had reached a new level. "Love and War" is the song that describes my feelings of love for him. My life has thrown some serious curve balls and I have learned strength in major ways. I had a lot of turns and corners, and through it all, I could not understand how I made it through. Then I realized it was God who gave me the strength and he carried me through to where I was able to walk on my own, but he has never left my side.

Trials and tribulations have no boundaries or limits, nor do they have a type. It comes when it wants to and can leave behind all types of damages that have to be repaired or rebuilt. I chose to expose my life and share my truths because we all have faced hard or difficult times in life. I chose to expose the truths of my life because through every difficult thing I have experienced, there has always been a lesson to learn, and I have had my fair share of struggles. Drugs, money, prison, domestic violence and loads of money, I have experienced it all. Although the end results nearly ended my life.

It was only God and man-made machines that kept me alive for the three months that I laid in a coma. When the doctors had a very low probability of surviving, the devil tried to take from me, but God did not agree. I am not at all complaining about the cards I was dealt with. I have learned to embrace all my struggles because throughout it all, I have learned strength that I never knew I had. I was able to find myself and build a deeper faith.

It was never an easy task; there were a lot of ups and downs, and I had to start over like a newborn baby. I was a grown adult who had reverted back to infancy, having to relearn everything that I already once knew. At the age of 25, my life ended, and then three months later, a Phoenix was born. I had gotten a second chance at life. I know I could not change the past or do it all over again and make it better, but it allowed me to think and make different decisions, and it allowed me to try and rebuild what was broken. It was never simple, but with God giving me strength, I was able to prevail and overcome the things that the devil tried to stop. All odds were against me, but I never allowed that to stop or slow my progress. Dealing with all the obstacles, I even had thoughts of ending it all. It seemed like an easier way out, but my spirit would not allow it. My faith and my strength grew an immense amount and carried me through the fire. I lived it, I experienced it, and I survived it. I chose to expose my truth and tell a story of a Phoenix being born. Because I am someone who has had trying times, to say the least, but God has given me a second chance in life. I feel like with my life, the lessons that I have learned, and the strength that I gained, I believe it was my purpose to share a story of a life filled with difficulties. I have learned without trials and tribulations, I would not have become the woman I am shaping up to be. Turns out, I like the woman I am becoming. I have experienced death, and I survived.

I hope that sharing my story may have some effect on anyone who just feels like throwing up their hands and giving up, who thinks life is too hard. I learned that what happened to me, happened, but it does not define me. My life may have been filled with troubles, but those troubles also defined me and made me who I am and who I am becoming.

In this book, I do not want to only share a life of turbulence and rocky roads. I want to tell my story because I am someone who has seen death. I was knocking on death's door, and luckily, no one answered. God had made a detour route for me, and he redirected my path. Literally having to start life all over from the beginning at the age of 25, the journey to rebuild and refurbish the old version of myself.

PART 1

CHAPTER 1

I was born a very stubborn baby. My due date was originally July 15, but I ended up coming nine days later, born on July 24. My mother was on work release when I decided to go in, make my final overdue awaited entrance, and be welcomed into the world. Once we arrived, my mother, Victoria, was rushed up to the maternity floor, and not soon after a couple of grunts and pushing, there I was, a little baby with a little alfalfa hair sticking straight up! I was welcomed as Janisha Scott. Victoria and I shared a couple of bonding days together, but then it was time for her to finish her time. She gave me one last kiss, and she was gone!

***

As for me, I went to stay at a couple of different family members' houses, including my daddy and my aunt Barbara. I stayed with my daddy for three months until we moved again, and when I said "we," it was not just me. I have one brother and three sisters, and we all go in chronological order, starting with my sister 'Shawnita,' who is the oldest, then my sister 'Quita' a few years later, then my brother James, followed by my sister Jasmine and a year later, there I was!

***

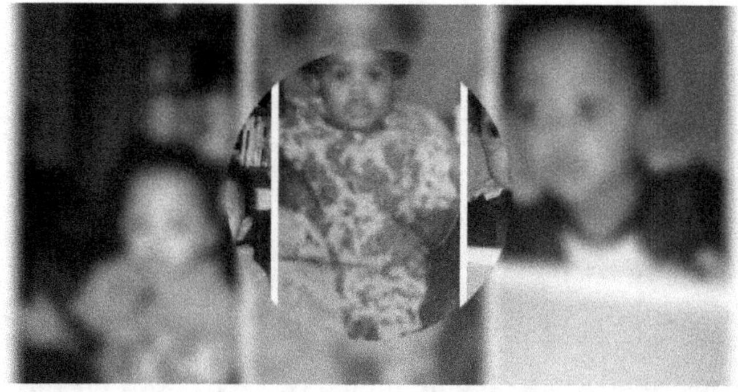

We were taken to a group shelter called "The Home Of The Innocence." My sister Nita was almost aged out of the group home, so she was almost on her own, but we enjoyed the time we had together. Soon, 'Nita' aged out, so that was the last time we ever saw her. As for the remaining siblings, we were still up for grabs. For me and my sister Jasmine, we automatically were a pair because we were 15 months apart, so that was a good deal. You could not take one without the other!

***

All the siblings were fostered from left to right; that was our home for years. We were being separated so fast, and often, it felt like we were being rented from different families over and over again. At this point, we hardly saw each other again. Occasionally, we would spend time together until it finally ended. First, it was Nita, then it was James, and then Quita was the next to go. It was left to the duo sisters now. We stayed there for a couple of months. There are two foster families I can recall that left a memory.

Ms. P (story time) (1990-1995)

Ms. P was also known as the 'switch' lady; she had no problem with telling one of us kids to go get a switch and laying marks on our skin! Jasmine and I were not alone; she shared a household full of other foster kids. We all shared two rooms filled with bunk beds. We were in one room with other kids. We had four beds, two-bed sets on each wall.

It was a household of kids, so it was kind of inevitable not to get into trouble! There were several occasions we both met the power of the switch! She would tell us, "Go out there and get a good switch and tear all the leaves off and bring it back to her," and we would do as told. We used to run and hide under beds, but to no avail. We still got our legs tapped anyways.

On this particular night, after dinner, it was time for a good bath. It was bedtime. We all filed in as usual and headed to bed. Once all was quiet, later on in the night, we began hearing someone talking and someone frantically moving around the room. It appears someone had peed on the bed, and they tried to cover it up by throwing the sheets on the floor in the middle. After covering up their crime, they tried to find something to replace the bed sheet with. They were causing a lot of attention because of all the noise that was being made, and then light fussing came. The stained peed-on sheets were invisible at this point until Ms. P could be heard coming down the hall. Jasmine and I were in our bed, and we acted like we were asleep when she walked into the room. We played asleep until the light switch was turned on, forcing us to "wake up." We tried to view the whole thing underneath the blankets! Ms. P walked in to see what the fuss was all about, and she was mad, having been awakened. We remained in bed while Ms. P entered the room. She walked around before she noticed the sheets in the middle of the floor mixed in with a few other items on the floor. No one was safe now when she ordered everyone to get up and answer the mysterious sheet's identity. Because of all the denying and semi-false accusations, it became a battle. When Ms. P had about enough, she just told us all to get up, and she already had her switch in her hands. She came prepared, knowing that we were all about to get tagged. Then, finally, someone broke the silence, and our legs were saved! We remained living there for a while before we were back.

***

We stayed with this one family for a short period of time, but I remember this story because it left a funny memory!

This family was short-lived, but the experience was one that I will always remember! This family was financially blessed; they lived in a really expensive neighborhood with big houses and nice cars in the driveways. The family consisted of just four people: the mother, the dad, a son and a daughter. The daughter was the oldest sibling, and the boy was a toddler, so he was closer to our age group. One night, we had bath night, and the three small ones got to bathe together. After washing ourselves, we were allowed to play in the water with the toys, and everything was going well. As the bubbles began to disappear, we began to see the water more clearly, and after we began picking up all the toys, we were left with a little surprise! The son had pooped while we were in the bath. Jasmine and I began screaming until our foster parents came in to see what was the matter, and after we showed them that there was a piece of poop floating in the water. We were there for a little while before they realized it was not a good fit.

***

Mr & Mrs. S Family, 1996

I can still remember when a short, yellow and plump lady walked in and when she walked out with us, following right behind her as we started getting into a white minivan. We stopped at the convenience store, and after picking up a few goodies, we headed to our new foster home.

Once we were there, we were introduced to the husband, who was sitting in his favorite recliner chair. There were also other foster kids. It was a house full, but it was also a household of fun and mystery. We kids were being switched in and out of the foster home so much that as soon as we thought we found a good option, the next day, they were gone and even though the kids were moving in and out, Jasmine and I remained there. Mrs. and Mr. S had a son and daughter in -in-law who came by a lot. We saw them regularly. They were current visitors. Over time, we began to become close with the family. Visits became more frequent, and over nights became more frequent. It was starting to feel like family.

Adoption "1997"
I am in the red shirt, and Jasmine is in the blue.

We started getting very close with the family, and in 1997, we were officially adopted into the household. My foster parents became our grandparents. Our ages were seven & eight. We now have a family life. Jasmine was the tidy sister, and I was the messy child. In the beginning years, Jasmine and I shared rooms until we were in our teen years. I was a very mischievous child growing up. I stayed in trouble. Jasmine was the good child, and I was the "other." I was not a straight-A student at all; I just made it to C or D average.

CHAPTER 2

I grew up in a Jehovah's Witness household. It was my religion growing up. I followed it but not devoutly. It was difficult growing up with certain restrictions. I didn't understand it entirely, but since then, I have grown to learn. There were a lot of restrictions that I did not always follow. I remember we took a trip to the "Big Apple" for a week to see a lot of spiritual landmarks within the Jehovah's Witnesses community, and I was able to see a lot of other things like Times Square. I also went to The Statue Of Liberty, and that's where I learned that it's deadly to throw a penny off the top of the statue. Even though I never found out, I'm still curious. New York was so busy and fast-paced; there was a whole lot going on there at one time. We saw a man who was riding his bike on the busy streets of New York City when a cab just casually hit him, and the traffic proceeded as usual. The traffic never slowed or stopped. Luckily, the man was alright, but I learned that New York City was ruthless!

*****

We've taken trips to Florida countless times, enjoying all the rides at the major theme parks. That's where I first learned that my body doesn't do well in the heat. I remember we were in a long waiting line to get on the newest "Back to the Future" ride. The line was long, but we were so excited to try the roller coaster, so we waited. When we finally got close to the ventilated air-conditioned entrance, everything went black, and with a "Thump,"...I passed out from heat exhaustion right before we entered. Needless to say, I never got to experience that ride!

-2000's-

As a family, we would take many trips all over the place, and I got to see a bunch of different places! The best vacation we ever took was a 7-Day Cruise to the West Caribbean islands. It was beautiful to see how other countries and worlds lived. It really was something to see. The driving, especially, was scary with the way we were up in high areas, rocky, jagged areas, and they drove on the opposite sides of the road, and they drove crazy, but it was my best and favorite vacation. It was so much fun!

That was a once-in-a-lifetime experience. I only wish I had pictures! My sister Jasmine was not on this trip because she had moved out.

CHAPTER 3

March – 2006 High school 11 grade (age 16-17)

The first time we actually reconnected with our siblings was a wild one.

Sitting in our separate classrooms, Jasmine and I sat endlessly listening to whatever the teacher was talking about when a call was made to both of our respective classrooms. It was a call from our principal, Ms. B, who then gave the instructions for Jasmine and me to come to her office. When I got the memo from my teacher that I was called to our principal's office, I had no clue that Jasmine was also called to the office. My first thought was, "Oh, what did I do now'? I wasn't the best student. I was known for getting in trouble.

Once in the office, I saw Jasmine. We were perplexed, and we couldn't figure out why we "both" had to be in the office "together." We had no clue as we were finally being called to her office. In utter confusion, we continued to walk back to her office. Once we were in her office, we sat down in some chairs facing her. She asked us a very odd question, "If we had a brother?" We told her, "Yes, we did." She then asked us what his name was. "Okay, weird question," We thought, and without even thinking, we said our adopted brother's name. When that name did not match with the name she had, she asked us again, and this time, we said that we did have another brother. It had been around 13-14 years since we saw any of our biological siblings. Her next few words took us by unbelievable surprise; she asked, "Do y'all have another brother? We answered, "Yes, we do." After being super confused, Jazzy and I exchanged puzzled looks. We then added, "Yeah, we do, but we haven't seen him or them since we were kids. Ms. B then asked us, "What his name was," and we said, "James." Ms. B then said the words that I will never forget, "Well, he is here." In utter disbelief, we began to follow her. We walked into the room, and standing there was a handsome boy. Now, this story was really weird. Even though we did notice we did share a striking resemblance, but nothing clicked yet. With further visual detection, we couldn't shake the fact that something about this guy stood out. He finally said, "I'm your brother, James!" Hold on, did this guy just say he was our brother?" Once the initial shock wore off, the room became misty as our eyes filled with tears. We immediately realized it was actually our brother James! That's why he looked so familiar. We all immediately huddled together and shared a very emotional, overwhelming hug! It was a good feeling to be hugging our actual birth family. We finally sat down and began talking, asking all types of questions like "How did you know? And how'd you know where to find us"? He said, "I had a session with our cousin in my science class." She also has some very distinctive features that were on my mother's side. Her name is Ki.... So, you mean to tell me that this whole school year,

I was sitting next to my cousin and did not have a clue? That explains the vibe I had with her the entire school year.

We all sat around and talked, catching up on how life was while growing up. We were starting to get carried away when we heard a knock on the door. It said that it was time to wrap it up. Even though it seemed like time had flown, we had to leave. We reluctantly got up, but we weren't ready to split up after all. It had been more than a decade since we had been in each other's presence. We exchanged information and one last embrace before it was time for us to separate.

Once we were done, we were dismissed back to our classes. We were on cloud nine when floating back to our rooms!

(Jasmine had a cellphone, and that's how we would keep in contact with our siblings).

CHAPTER 4

Quita's Graduation Party

~2006~

Through it all, I could always depend on my sister Jasmine. No matter what we may have been going through, I knew I could always count on her, regardless. She was and is always in my corner, right/wrong/indifferent! She's always had my back!

****

Jasmine was 17, and I was 16. We were living at home, but Jasmine and I were up to no good. We were planning a mischievous plan! We had made secret plans to go to a graduation party thrown by our biological and at this party, we would be meeting our family members for the very first time.

****

Jasmine and I had a neighborhood friend. We planned on saying that we were going to "Kentucky Kingdom" (which is an amusement park.) We even went as far as saying that a friend's brother was going to be the one who would be the one taking us back and forth! Sounds simple, right? Well, in all honesty, my sister had a "boyfriend" who was going to be the one taking us to the party and bringing us back.

Now, it was time to execute the plan!

We started walking down to our friend's house, and the plan was in full effect. After that, we said our goodbyes and walked down the street to our friend's house. The boyfriend was already in position down there, waiting for us.

***

Once we were in the truck, we were in the clear. We headed down, playing and listening to music, getting ready for an introduction. Our nerves were fine until we reached the party. They were in full effect, but we had to pull it together and hopped out of the truck, just to be greeted by our brother James, who then asked, "Are y'all ready"? We answered, all nervous, "Yeah." This would actually be the first time meeting our biological family members for the first time, so yes, our nerves were on ten, but we had come this far. There was no turning back now.

***

James then began walking around, introducing us to different parts of the family members. We got to meet a lot of aunts and uncles, cousins, and the whole shebang! It was now time to meet the woman of the day, our sister Quita, and we finally made it over to her. We held a long and loving embrace before we all sat down, and for the next couple of hours, we sat and talked continuously. We ate occasionally, talking more and more with the family before we realized that all good things must come to an end. It was getting late, and we knew it meant that the amusement park would be closing soon, so it was time to get our game face on and press play!

We slowly said our goodbyes, exchanging information, and even though we really didn't want to leave, it was time to make our way back home. It was game mode on!*** While driving back home, we began to go over our game plan. Getting closer to the house, Jasmine made a phone call to the stand-friend who was on standby waiting for the call to check and see if there was any commotion going on.

When Jasmine got off the phone, she said that "J" informed that my mom and siblings had come down there to see if we were back yet and where we were at. Luckily "J" was home alone, so there were no cars in the driveway, so when they came knocking and ringing the doorbell 'J' just ignored it and stayed upstairs in her room.

****

Now, pulling into our neighborhood, Jasmine and I were seated low near the floorboard of the truck, but we were positioned with our heads at a level where we could still look out of the window. 'Our house was the first in the neighborhood. We were still sitting low, and we noticed that our house was calm; there were no lights on except for a small lamp in the front. Everything else seemed calm.. until we drove a little further. We saw our mother and two siblings walking down from the direction from where the friend lived.

We just made sure we were low enough in the truck as we rode through. Since the truck windows were tinted, we could see out, but they couldn't see in. We sat in the truck. We figured we would just wait it out in the truck they knew nothing about and wait until we thought they were close to home. We began going over our game plan, which was, "We were at the amusement park, and her brother brought us home. It was time for us to escape unseen and unheard. We then went into game mode. We crossed over the street to where our house was at the other end. We started walking, slowly becoming aware of the situation we got ourselves in, but we played it cool till the end. Now, reaching our house, we were like 6 or 7 houses away when we saw my mother and sister just got back to our driveway. We immediately slowed walking down for a bit, and then we continued with our pace. By this time, my mother was in the house, so we continued as planned. We were just a couple of houses away from our driveway when, out of nowhere, someone came from behind, jumped on my back, and tried to take me down. I was trying not to go down and get grass stains on my white outfit. When we went to the graduation party, we both wore our airbrushed outfits. I wore a blue outfit while Jasmine wore red. I read from that song from "Dem Franchize Boyz, "Oh, I think they like me!" I was definitely not trying to get any grass stains or anything on my outfit. No matter all my fights, I started to grow weak. He almost had me down on the ground when, out of nowhere, Jasmine came running up and gave him a taste of his own medicine. She jumped on his back, and they struggled until our mother came out and made them get off each other. Then we headed into the house. Standing in the entryway of the house, Jasmine and I began our story about our trip to the Kentucky Kingdom that remained a secret until

now......sorry!

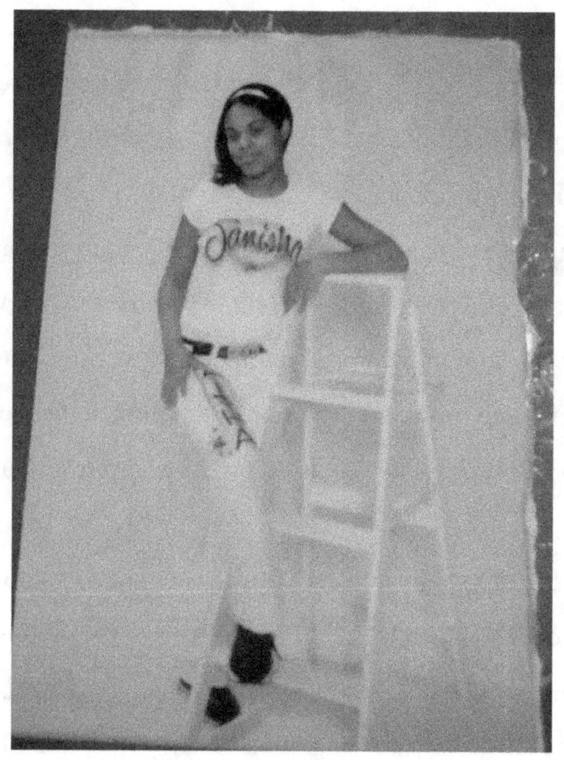

(This is the outfit my spring pictures "2007")

PART 2

CHAPTER 1
2008

At the age of 17, I ran away from my home because of some inconsolable differences. Out of respect for the parties involved, I will not comment on what I felt could have been handled differently. I left home and entered the real world, still wet behind the ears. I had no clue what I was going to do or where I was going to go. I have been in contact with my siblings, so I reached out to my sister, Shawnita, who offered me a place to stay. There, I was finally able to grow and build a relationship with my sister after decades of not knowing each other. It took me a minute to fully get adjusted, but I did. We really got to know each other over smoking sessions! My sister Quita was also on her school break.

Quita and I discovered that we both shared the same funny bone, so we were always on some goofy stuff! This one time, Quita and I were sitting at home, smoking. We were feeling good and very bored. There were kids out front playing, and we decided to have some fun. So, we went to Walmart and found a BB gun, a small pellet gun. We took the gun home and set up a shop, hiding behind a couch. We dimmed the blinds, and the window was already cracked. We started shooting the pellet gun at the group of kids, and they had no clue where it was coming from. They were looking left and right but could not find the shooter. We were even going upstairs in the hallway and looking out the window blasting. It was so funny!

While living there, I found a job at Walmart as a cashier, and with everything that was going on in my life, I did not complete high school. It was supposed to be my graduation year, "2008." I was also in the process of trying to secure my first apartment.

While living with my sister, I remember there was a boy in the neighborhood who was actually affiliated with the same religion. We were past friends. Fast forward to some years, I ran into him and began a relationship. He was my first experience with domestic violence; he would slap and choke me. That's as far as domestic violence went with him. I stayed with him for the first couple of years of my being out in the world. When I secured my first apartment, it was time for changes to be made. And I eventually parted ways with him and took to the world on my own.

CHAPTER 2
"Do You Do X-Rated Texting?"

While working, I saw and rang up a lot of people, and not one of them phased me until I met a guy named "Mr." and he opened my eyes. He introduced me to what the "Real world" was. Growing up with my religion, I was not used to the real world reality. I was just instructed to stay away from evil ...my blinders were about to reveal what life was. Mr was a hustler, and I loved his business-mentality side. I love his wisdom as well as his gangster and gentleman sides. He was everything in one!

"Do you do x-rated texting?" That was the first thing Mr said to me, and that was the start of something new ...... I was new in the world and in need of guidance, and with that one question, my eyes were opened. Even though Mr. had his own thing going on, it did not stop me. I was young, fresh, and impressive in the world when he took me under his wings for 5.6 years. He was older than me by a decade, which meant he had wisdom and knowledge, and that wisdom and knowledge is something I yearned to learn. For almost 6 years, I played my position in the background while learning a lot. I cannot begin to tell all the different stories and experiences. It is a story for another time. From a bottom bitch to a madam, I had my hands in all kinds of pots. I had touched and ran into all kinds of money and had done all kinds of things until the day I got a wake-up call.

****

February 18, 2010

With a series of bad decisions, it all finally caught up with me. I have traveled across state lines, I have traveled to a couple of different spots on the map to go and secure large portions of marijuana, then come back to the home fronts, and just continue the recycling process over and over again. Securing the amount that we did required the supplier to be armed and prepared on a Washington DC level.

Mr, our driver, and I would take trips to Arizona and Texas. We would leave the state with a bunch of currency and then return with the products! We made a few runs, and they were all successful trips. Our driver made sure everything was up to code with the limit and law to ensure no hiccups. We had made these trips before, so we were familiar with the journey just as long as we continued to follow the protocols. Outside of just burning gas mileage, that was not our only source of income; we always had some side business going on that guaranteed income.

Chapter 3

It was supposed to be just another trip, easy in and easy out. I was on the floor of the back seat, while Mr was on top where he had little more room. He was overhead, on the top floor, and I was on the bottom floor. Underneath the bottom floor was a secret compartment where we had our money. One day, we were driving through Amarillo, Texas, Carson County lines. On this particular day, we were lying down. Mr and I were in the backseat sleeping, and the driver kept the truck on cruise control mode, always 5 miles under the speed limit, just to be safe. We were on the side of the highway with cars zooming past.

While we were sleeping, we were suddenly awakened by our driver saying, "Oh s***, I think we're getting pulled over! The way it happened was out of this world. The police directed us to get out of the truck and face down, lying on the ground face-first. They began asking us questions, 'Do we have any weapons or anything that could incriminate us?' We lifted our heads and replied, "No." We were not too worried about the money because it was hidden under the floorboard. After searching for a few minutes, they found the hidden compartment where the money was stashed. The moment they saw all the money, they immediately pulled out their guns and pointed them directly at us. They began asking us more questions, but we already had a whole story prepared about why we had that money. But in the end, we were arrested and taken to a barnyard/office that they claimed their office was at.

The barnyard had nothing but a police truck, some tables, and folding chairs. We were all directed to sit in the chairs, still handcuffed but now to the chairs. We began watching them as they were in "omg" over the amount of money they confiscated. They were gleaming with pride over the big arrest they made and were taking pictures with it. And by the way they were taking pictures like it was a big bust. The police then discussed what they would do with us. No matter what we told them, they were not buying it. According to them, Mr was the muscle, our diver was our diver, and I was the "middle guy." In the end, "they called it as they saw it" except for no proof other than money. It became circumstantial.

They added up the total sum, totaling $55,110. They were able to run up on bundles of money, but there were no drugs, which is what they were looking for. Unbeknownst to us, I-70 was the known drug route. They found a bottle of pills that were prescribed to Mr, but it did not stop them from adding that as a false misdemeanor charge. As far as the money, that was a whole different story. They had it stacked up in a zip-lock evidence bag.

Once they were done taking their evidence, we were then taken to the real sheriff's office. We were processed and booked, and within a couple hours, we were bailing out to face this mess we got ourselves into.

CHAPTER 4

Texas was in no hurry to fully prosecute the; The court process lasted over a year and a half. But life had to continue, and it did.

Through our waiting period, I began to get restless. I had gotten to the point where I was no longer interested in being "the side." Watching Mr go home every night and lay his head on another pillow while I could not was not a role I wanted anymore. With Mr helping me realize my value and worth, we decided to friend zone each other, but we still remained super close friends. Love and loyalty are stronger than any addiction!

~2011~

It was late spring when my best friend Ace and I decided to put on some cute clothes and walk to a corner store. My apartment building was right next to an expressway entrance, so you never know what you might see. So, we had to make sure we looked cute before we left.

***

As we were walking back from the store, a black jeep slowed down a little bit and then pulled over to the side and later parked up the street. As we got closer to the jeep, the driver began yelling, trying to get our attention. We decided to reply with a funny remark to "the catcall" that he said as we crossed the street to talk face to face. After a few minutes, it was confirmed that the "catcall" was directed to me.

After exchanging some information, we continued on our walk back, feeling accomplished!

Things started out great. I can remember the early dating stage. I would either be at my apartment or over at my friend's house, and he would always come through and hang out with me and bring me whatever I needed during his "break time." We would hang out a lot and spend time over my apartment or his trapper house.

*****

I remember the first time he hit me. We were in the upstairs apartment that we shared and had a disagreement about something. I do not remember what it was about, but I remember he took his palm and swung his hand backward. The next thing I experienced was a stinging sensation across my cheek. He had smacked fire from my face, and I couldn't remember my reaction, but I believe I was more shocked than in pain. After a few hours, all was forgiven, and things continued as usual.

CHAPTER 5

The life that I shared with him was "Everything that glitters is not gold." On the outside, it was every young girl's dream to be with the hottest guy in the city. Climbing that ladder on a mid-level, he was known in the areas all around town, but that was not the reason I stayed with him. I had honest, genuine -true-to-the-heart feelings for him. I endured the pain because I believed that if I proved I was strong enough, my love and feelings for him would prevail. I wanted to show him that I loved him. Things looked good from the outside, but on the inside, they were broken.

CHAPTER 1
Adultism

There I was, half-naked, crouched down in a not-so-clean bathroom.

I had just run away from the home we shared with nothing on but a ripped-up muscle shirt. Luckily, my run wasn't far from where I was going. I ran to a nearby restaurant's bathroom and luckily found it empty.

I went to the sink and started wiping all the blood from my face and body. I had gashes and cuts all over my face and body. I looked like I got into a fight and came out a total mess. I went back to find a stall and found one. It was a handicapped stall, so I had room. I couched down because I had no panties on. I began thinking that I needed to come up with a plan because I just couldn't sit in the bathroom and always run. It's that four-letter word "love" that always made me stay.

I had just endured another fight. He had put the smackdown on me (again). At this point, I have lost count of the reasons why he does what he does. It was a pity to know that I was sitting in a dirty bathroom with a ripped t-shirt, no panties, and no shoes, which was not a pleasant run, rocks, glass, and all!

PART 3

My train of thought was halted mid-way when I heard the door creep open. I immediately went into panic mode, thinking, could it be him because we didn't live far from where I was? Luckily, it was a restaurant employee, and I'm guessing it was because they saw a half-naked girl run into their establishment. She waited for the restroom to be empty before she asked me, "Is everything alright?" I told her that I was okay, but then I also asked if they had a phone that I could use. The employee left, and I resumed my thoughts. Before I could get into deep thought, the door opened again; it was her with the phone. She handed it to me through the door, and she could tell by the way I looked that something was wrong.

I immediately called my sister Jasmine. She's always had my back. After ringing many times, she finally answered. I gave her a quick rundown of what just took place. I told her where I was, and that's all I had to say. She was on her way immediately. I got out of the stall and checked myself in the mirror when the employee returned, and I handed back the phone to her. She noticed how I was in trouble, and she also offered to call the police. I told her that I was okay and had a family member coming to pick me up. "What can I say? I was love-struck". The employee left back out, not believing I was okay.

I sat there, nervous as ever, as I waited for my sister to come. Jasmine lived in the next state over, so I knew it would take a little minute before she got to me. My waiting period left me anxious and nervous because we did not live far from where I was at. I stepped back out of the bathroom stall for a quick second. I did not want any-one to see me. I went to look at my beat-up face and body. I had a black eye and a red eye. My nose was bleeding, and my lips were all busted up. I looked at myself again, and it was such a pity. No matter how much I loved him, I had to ask myself, "Is this what love is?"

15-20 minutes had passed. My sister was finally here. Thank goodness! She got out of her car and noticed the police car pulling in as well. She jetted her way to the door and got inside before the police came in. Luckily, the police were still in their car. As soon as she got in the restroom and looked at me, she got upset, but she tended to my care. She handed me a bigger shirt, and we started quickly talking about what had happened while getting me good enough to walk out. Once we were done, we first cracked the door open to make sure we were clear enough to walk out normally and sneak away before the police came in. But it didn't quite work like that. The police met us at the door when we opened it. In that moment, I thought that it was about to go down. The officer began asking me questions concerning what was going on by looking at my posture and face. He knew some-thing was wrong. I had my other cuts and bruises covered up by the long shirt.

He began asking me questions about what actually took place. I lied to him and said I just had a girl fight. I told him my sister was here to pick me up and take me away to her home. The police were skeptical, but in the end, they released us, and we were free to go. On our way back to Jasmine's house, we had a long conversation. She was making sense, but you could not tell my head or heart anything. A couple of days later, I was back on the phone with him, arranging to go back home.

(I was really in love no matter which way I looked at it. In my heart and mind, I really felt that I loved him, and I really believed that he would change his ways once he saw that I would ride with him no matter what. I was in for a rude awakening!) I had marks and bruises that I constantly made excuses for, and I was finding myself getting numb to the abuse.

****

I was still able to keep in contact with Mr for a while until jealousy and "insecurities" popped up, and that was the end of our public relationship.

Even though Mr and I decided to keep things on a professional level, I was only able to remain in contact with him if we had to run across each other's path. Of course, he knew we remained in contact to a level where he would know our interactions. Mr never lost his concern for my well-being. One way or another, he always made sure I was okay because he knew that I was in a toxic relationship and my environment was toxic. *(The Texas trail still continued...)*

CHAPTER 2
Memory

I cannot recall the timeline, but it is in my memory as something I will never forget. I remember he had beat me up really bad once again, and what I can remember of it was after he beat me up, I was laid out in my apartment in the back room of my bedroom on the floor. I remember I heard him on the telephone, saying, "Come pick this b**** up. I just beat her up." Before he left the door, I did not know who was on the phone. I was hardly conscious, but I remember I was still lying on the floor. A couple of minutes later, I heard the back door to my apartment being jiggled. My first thought was that maybe he wasn't done yet. He was coming back to finish what he started. At that time, I did not have the energy or strength to get up, so I remained on the floor. When the door was opened, it was Mr. He had called Mr to give that message. This is one thing I will always remember because when Mr found me on the floor in my bedroom, firstly, he secured and checked the premises to make sure everything was okay before he attended to my needs. I remember sitting up on the side of my small sofa in my bedroom. Mr went to the restroom, gathered washcloths, wet them down, and then came back to tend to my needs.

THROUGH THE FIRE

*****

For days into weeks, I have learned to become a master at hiding my hurt and pain. To the naked eye, everything was nice, but behind it all, it was a love story turning into a horror story....

We may have had some very good times, such as taking trips to Florida. Our trip to Miami had good intentions but ended in its"typical" way. We would always go on extravagant shopping sprees and trips, but behind the good always sat the bad. I have been hurt to the core. I literally felt like my body was snapping in half like I could feel my bones ripping from one another. I have had aches and pains with their own aches and pains. There were times when I honestly felt I was about to die. The injuries were so severe. It was no average black eye and a red cheek. My womb was like some images out of a horror room. I was not a makeup wearer outside of the basic eyeliner and mascara, but I learned how to apply makeup to cover up and hide the areas from other people.

Even though I had become a master of hiding, there was still one person who knew everything that I could not hide from, and that was Jasmine. She was there every step of the way. She encouraged me the most to move on and to make better choices, but you could not tell my heart anything.

~Memory~

He drove me way up in the woods, where it was a haunted house on the top. When we got halfway, he stopped the car, dragging me out into the grassy area where he proceeded to choke me, and when

41

I lost consciousness, I don't know for how long I remained there before finally waking up with HIM in the car just smoking a cigarette and watching me.

CHAPTER 3

~March-April, 2016~

This particular story has its major downs, but it was rewarded with a gift in the end.

It was a beautiful day when we decided to go to the mall and do some shopping. We decided to load up in his black Camaro and hit the road. As we were in the car, we jammed to some tunes as we headed to the mall. On the way, it was good, nice and friendly, listening to music and just enjoying the good vibes that we shared. We headed inside the mall. In my mind, I already knew the routine, eyes down or on him, and I followed suit just to keep the peace and vibe. I don't know what went on in his mind. If I looked at anyone, he would consider flirting or sending signals, so I kept my eyes down or on him just to keep the peace. We went in and out of a couple of good stores. I went to my favorite store, Victoria's Secret and made a couple of purchases before we were on to our next journey! We went in and out of a bunch of stores, some of this and some of that. Then we rounded up to the last store, and their store definitely was the last stop!

Luckily, the store was empty, and outside, the workers were also females. I was in the clear, so I thought everything was good, until it wasn't. We separated, and while we were looking at clothes, I found a couple of items that I liked. I picked them up and headed back up to the front to get to Him. Then, just like clockwork, three guys and one girl walked in. I knew it was better to get up to him fast. And I was back with him; I stayed glued to him, focused on his eyes and whatever he was looking at. The three guys separated, but there were two guys not too far away from where He was. I got back to him right on time and remained glued to him. The other two guys were coming closer to where we were. They were just looking at clothes over by us. Everything was going well until we realized the two guys were close, and one of them was coming closer, looking at the clothes on the rack nearby. That's when things changed.

I knew what to do, and that was to follow the routine. I kept my eyes down the whole time (the floor was amazing). Then, in one fateful moment, he asked me a question, and I had to look up to answer him. My eyes were focused on him the whole time my eyes were seeing his eyes, but it didn't matter. Apparently, that guy was right behind him, looking at the clothes on the rack, but I didn't pay him any attention. I saw him, but my focus was strictly on him. He had asked for my opinion, causing me to look in the direction that he was holding up his pickings. As I went to look up, I noticed that guy was close to HIM, but my focus was on Him. However, it didn't even matter at that point; he had already made up his mind. When it was time to pay for our clothes, there were two people behind the register. He was mad the whole time; he was fuming, so I knew this one was going to get ugly.

In actuality, I knew in my heart and soul that I never looked at anyone. I knew the consequences, but that's what he thought could not be changed. Finally, when we got to the front register, and I was holding my clothes, he decided that I wasn't going to get any clothes (bummer). So, he paid for his clothes only, and we were out of the store. To add insult to injury, he made me carry his bags out. The ride back home was an uncomfortable one. It did not feel the same as it had been when we had gone to the store; it was not all that good. Once in the car, he wasted no time in threatening me, telling me what I should look forward to when we get back to the comfort of our home. He was describing all the torture he was going to inflict upon me. He constantly tried to make it known what I should look forward to. He started out violently, telling me what he was going to do to me because I was "supposedly" looking at another guy, but I'd say once again that I was not. No matter what I said, it went in one ear and out the other, basically on deaf ears. Then, out of nowhere, I got a heavy SMACK across my face. I went down in pain, soothing my cheek. I knew there was more to come. The ride home felt like we were never going to reach our destination because hits and blows were flying all over me, on the passenger side. He was still able to get some good blows in while he was driving. I didn't know what he had in his mind, but I knew this was just a warm-up because once he was enraged, it was nothing simple.

After we got home, there was no time for pleasantries. He began attacking me, tagging to the legs and the arms with forceful hits. Then he went for my entire body, tagging me left, right, up, and down. I was basically in the fetal position, trying to protect my bare legs. And just when I thought it was finally over. I guess he had some more energy to do his one last move on me. He brought his shoe right down on my left side, slamming straight into my ribs. At that moment, I instantly knew something inside me had broken. I remained there on the floor in pain. I was totally flat out in a cradled position. I was in excruciating pain at that point. I felt like I was going in and out of consciousness, but I tried to keep it together. He was up on my bed, watching me with him, in pain with no care in the world. My body felt so broken that I came back down with every attempt I tried to get up. It was too hard, so I went back to the floor. He kept insisting on getting up, and I kept telling him, "I can't get up. It hurts."

I attempted to get up a couple more times, but the more I did it, the more I felt my body was tearing apart. Something was definitely wrong. He was getting irritated and annoyed. In his mind, he thought that I was acting and exaggerating and that he'd had enough. He took one more dig at me before he jerked me off the floor and ordered me to get up. When he did that, I felt my body broke, oh, like it was just gone at that point. I stumbled my way over to my bed and lay down because I knew I was hurt. I didn't know where, but I was definitely in pain. Before I knew, he left, and there I was, lying on my bed in excruciating pain. I lay there all night until the next day.

The next couple of days, things went on as usual. I gritted and bared my teeth the whole way through, but after a while, he noticed that I was in unbearable pain. He became my hood doctor, buying me prescription pills and ace bandages, wraps, and icy hot patches for my ribs.

Day in and Day out, we kept this procedure going until I couldn't take it anymore. My body was physically through. I kept telling him that I needed to go to the doctor's, but I knew he didn't want to take me to the hospital because it would raise suspicion on him. After a day or two, I started persistently asking him to go to the hospital. A day later, he agreed to take me. The next day, we geared up to go to the hospital, but before we left, we went over the story that would be 'I hurt myself because I was dancing with friends.' Of course, it wasn't the case at all, but whatever it took for me to go to see the doctor, it was what it was. Once we got all signed in and in the waiting area, we had a simple conversation, "putting on that fake life." After a while, it was finally time to be seen by the doctor. The doctor observed my ribs. He took a couple of notes and examined some more. He then went to his notes in the charts and noticed that I hadn't taken the urine test, so he asked me to go to the restroom and release. I was in a wheelchair, so I went to the stall, did my business, came out, and gave him my cup. From the test result, we learned that two of my ribs were badly sprained and that I was pregnant!!!

****

My life had spiraled out of control all the way to the bottom. I was involved with drug use during a critical time of my life. I did not want to tell this ugly truth of my life because I am not proud of it, but it is part of my truth. I dabbled in drug use for a couple of months, and there was no excuse. I was dealing with a lot (still not an excuse). I was crushing under the amount of pressure I was under while he was in jail at that time, but that did not prevent him from making terroristic and threatening phone calls to me when I was not doing anything. I was alleviating my pains with drugs. I was living in a drug-infested household while I was pregnant. My drug run lasted a few months until.......

CHAPTER 4

(I was still fighting my case in Texas. At this time, Mr. and I were very professional, with HIM monitoring my every interaction with him. Our court process lasted over a year and a half. I was finally sentenced to 4 years, but I was to serve one year only and the rest of the three years on parole.)

~Oct 4, 2016~

My son was born, but because my blood work was not clean, my son had to leave with my sister, Quita. He remained in her care while I handled my legal and violent relationship. I was very lucky and blessed to have my family step in and care for my child while I was trying to get myself together. Even though he was living with family, HIM and I kept trying to be a fixture in his life, and I was continuously hiding my bruises. He was between the ages of one and two when I was finally sentenced to serve one year in a Texas penitentiary. To this day, I am still trying to fix my mistakes with him. He was too young to understand what was going on.

***

(Memory)

My time in prison wasn't ideal in the least. A year was given to the state of Texas Department of Criminal Justice. I was miles and states away from my newborn child and my family. It was painful, but it was an outcome of the poor choices I made. I stayed to myself while I was there. I remained like a fly on the wall, observing the other inmates and getting to know who I could and couldn't have a vibe with.

I had made a few associates and made the best of my living situation, being housed with 28 other women who were all in there for numerous reasons. Money was kept in my account through HIM. Mr had put some money into my books when I first arrived. He acknowledged the sacrifice that I made for him and showed his gratitude the only way he could, which was by putting money on my books. And that was the last time we talked. I sat in the prison 23 hours a day and was only allowed 1 hour outside. I was surrounded by females only, and the only contact I had with a man for a year was not physical. I was seeing the male guards only.

'HIM' and I always communicated through the phone and in letters and J-pays emails. We always made sure to connect on every level. I also kept in touch with my father. He would be where I would be paroling once I was released. No matter the distance, the arguing and fighting continued. Some days were filled with love, while others were filled with pure rage about numerous things. I'm not ever claiming to be an angel. I had and have my flaws. I am not perfect, but the physical and mental abuse took its toll on me.

CHAPTER 5

****Release Date February 18, 2013****

THE LEAD UP

On June 1st, 2011, I pleaded guilty to a third-degree money laundering felony charge.

I served my time for one year before my release date, which was 18, 2013. They were waiting to pick me up, none other than HIM and his friend. They were there to take me away from a place I vow to never return to!

Once all the hugs and kisses were made between HIM and me, we quickly got in the car and decided to get out of that parking lot as fast as we could. As we were driving to the gas station, we were just talking about my experience of being "on the farm." We shared a few laughs as we were on our way to a gas station to buy some drinks and snacks and gas up before we got on the road later for the next day. (The guys had already gotten a room earlier when they arrived in Texas).

The guys entered the store after 'HIM' checked on me to see what I wanted. I had chosen to stay in the car and was fine with that. It felt so good to be just outside of the prison walls. I was happy to be looking at the bums on the street. I was just content with that view.

Within a few minutes, the guys were walking out with bags in their hands, and we were on the way to the hotel. I was excited to feel what I took for granted: a smooth shower. I would feel like hard water is not good all the time. I wanted to feel soft water cascade on my skin. Yeah! I was excited, to say the least.

***

Now, at the hotel, we gathered our belongings and went up to the room. I was so ready to take a shower! We chatted a bit after we got in the room about my prison experience, and then the friend knew what time it was. He excused himself and left the room to us. It was time for our private time. And boy, it was such a great private time. It was a year's worth of not having none, then finally being able to get some!

***

We had an amazing time. It was a year's worth of waiting for some strong man loving! We reached euphoria with each other for sure! Then it was time to clean up because right on time, the friend was back at the door, ready to come in, so I excused myself and went to the shower room.

***

I was getting out of the refreshing shower and looking in the mirrors when I noticed the guy's tone was rising, but I paid no heed. I proceeded to get dressed and get together. 10-15 minutes later, I heard the guys' voices rise again. They were not in a screaming match, but it was enough to get me alerted. The only thing I was thinking was, "I'm on parole. I could not have that, so I walked out of the bathroom, trying to see what was happening. I knew nothing to interfere with when two guys were going at it, and when they saw me, they calmed down. I don't know what happened from point A to point B. But the next thing I remember is I was being choked up with Force. I could feel my air supply being cut off. I could feel my eyes bulging out of my eye socket. I remained as strong as I could and kept trying to catch my breath. I was getting very lightheaded. He must have forgotten that I was on parole, which would have caused unnecessary attention for him and us to get jammed up. Luckily, his friend said, "Hey man, she's on parole. You can't do that s*** here." This knocked some sense into HIM, and he slowly began loosening his grip so I could catch my breath. We immediately felt we may have caused unwanted attention, so we decided to get out of the hotel and to Texas ASAP. We gathered all our belongings and headed out to the parking lot, trying to be unnoticed, and everything was all good until....

CHAPTER 6

We were walking to our car when......out of nowhere, the police came rolling deep into the parking lot. I believe there were two or three Jeep trucks and a police car. They came in so close, creating a whole scene. We proceeded as usual, acting oblivious to their approach. As we attempted to get in the truck, the police and detectives hollered over for us to stop us from getting in the vehicle. When the police arrived, he started asking us questions. However, we played smart and gave them false information. We were not going to tell them the real story, but we did let them know that they were there picking me up from prison, so that's why they were in Texas.

After a few more minutes of huddling up and talking, the next thing I knew, our car was being impounded for unclear reasons.

***

We were forced to take the Greyhound bus back home. "Yes, we were mad and couldn't understand why the car was impounded in the first place, but it was, and we were forced to take the Greyhound bus home." Coincidentally, we were left with just enough money to get back home." The police officer took us to the bus station.

***

Once our tickets were purchased, we had a good couple of hours before boarding the bus for that 17-hour trip back home.

We lollygagged around Carson County, Texas, for a bit, but the air was already thick. We were barely talking to one another.

CHAPTER 7

It was finally time to get on the bus, and they couldn't come sooner. We immediately headed to the front of the line. There were a couple of people in front of us, so our aim was to go straight to the back. Lucky for us, the other passengers sat up front as we loaded on, so we had the back seats all to ourselves. His friend got to one side of the long cushioned bench, and HIM and I were at the other end, where we were all laid up. At first, cuddled up, we were enjoying our ride so far....

***

And we're riding hours into the trip. HIM turned into Jekyll and Hyde because he switched on me and started talking recklessly, threatening me, and all that violent talk. In my mind, I'm not trying to hear that crazy talk, like I'm on parole for the next 4 years, so I definitely didn't need any foolishness, and I was just fresh out, so I decided it'd be best if I got up and move seats. Even though I was afraid of moving, but that's what I ended up doing. After a couple more threats, if I were to leave those seats, he planned on doing something to me once we got home. But I've had enough. I was scared, but I got up and walked to the front, feeling empowered, and stayed there until we reached our city. We did not exchange words at all. The guys went one way with their ride, which was his people. They left and went their separate ways. My daddy was there to pick me up because that's why I was paroled. It was nice to catch up with my daddy and talk to him. Over the next couple of days, I stayed with my daddy, getting into foolishness, and then I made the biggest mistake. I chose to lie to my father. I told him that a female friend of mine would pick me up and go out, but it was a lie. When, in all actuality, it was HIM coming to pick me up.

***

When I got the call saying he was out front, I put on my lying face and told my father that my girlfriend was there to pick me up. My daddy was in his room, so I didn't expect him to get up and see me off, but he did! I tried to make it out of the apartment before my daddy got up. I was already outside going down and walking to the car when my daddy opened the door. He noticed that I was getting in the car with HIM. And that was the last time I would ever be seen again. I became M.I.A for two and a half months before my body was found lying face down naked in the back of an alley in the back of a house. My body remained there for an unspecified amount of time when a bicyclist was riding through, and he noticed a naked body. He then flagged down a car driving pass and called the police.

When the police got the call, they had called it a possible overdose, but when they got to the scene, they changed the call to the homicide unit. However, after close observation, they noticed some life was left in me. I was left in grave condition, and then the race to save my life began. I was left in that alley for an unspecified amount of time, so I'm just glad that the passerby was able to notice and call for help.

sday June 31ʳˢᵗ, 2016 at approximately 0748 hours, Detective re
y of [redacted] Sexual Assault Nurse Examiner V. [redacted] of an
ing from the Fourth Division. Detective was notified that the
onscious on life support in the Emergency Department at Univ

CHAPTER 8

The way my family was notified about what had happened to me was wild. The police had no way to identify me. I was unrecognizable. They were not able to get a solid identity. Blood work was taken, and then from there, they were able to contact my adoptive parents first. After a few minutes, the police were told that they had not had any contact with me for years. The police then found my biological father's information, and when they contacted him, they did not lead on to what was going. They only informed him to stay put until they arrive. My dad had no clue what was going on. The detectives confirmed that he was my biological father before they delivered the bad news. They told him that he needed to come to the hospital to identify my body. He was able to identify me. Luckily I had a very distinct back tattoo that read "The Baddest Bitch ~ 1Huned~" I got that tattoo when I was 17, and I was feeling like that. Now I'm glad I decided on that young tramp stamp!

***

My dad stayed with me for a couple of days in the hospital until the detectives felt the need to place me in protective custody because of the level of intensity. At that time, I had no memory at all. And it drives me crazy to recall what took place over that two-and-a-half or three-month span of time. The detectives felt it was important to move me because of an incident where it was said that a guy walked in and lied about being my brother so he could go back and see me, but the detectives knew who my siblings were. I don't know what his motives were, but they were not taking any chances. I was all the more determined to find out so I could put it to rest. Today, I have to live with disabilities because of his actions. I want to know what happened in my past life so I can shut down that part of my old existence and begin to live my life and enjoy my existence on earth fully now.

I have been blessed with a second chance, and I just want to put an end to my previous life so I can fully enjoy this "2nd chance at life" the way it was intended for me to live out my dreams and purpose!

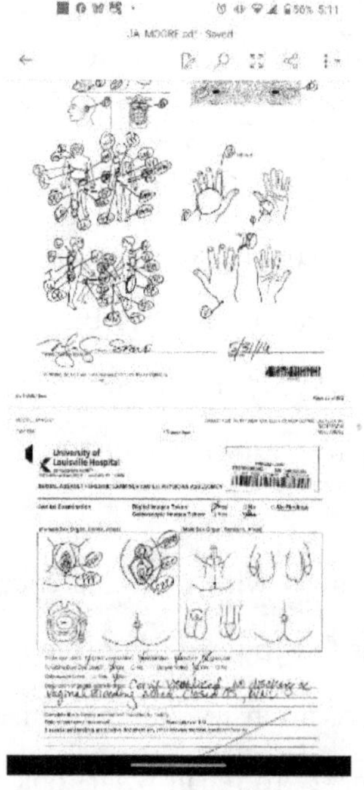

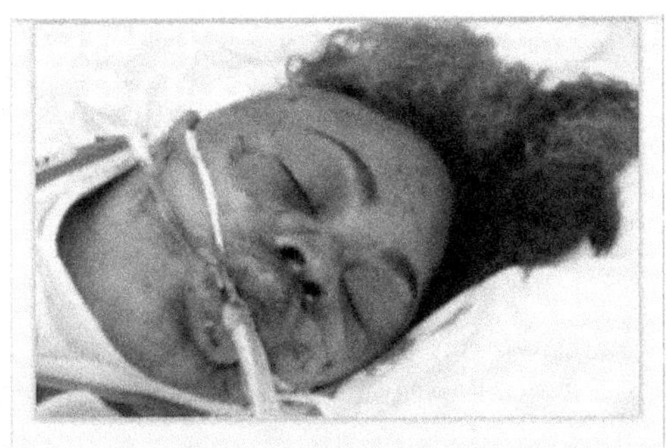

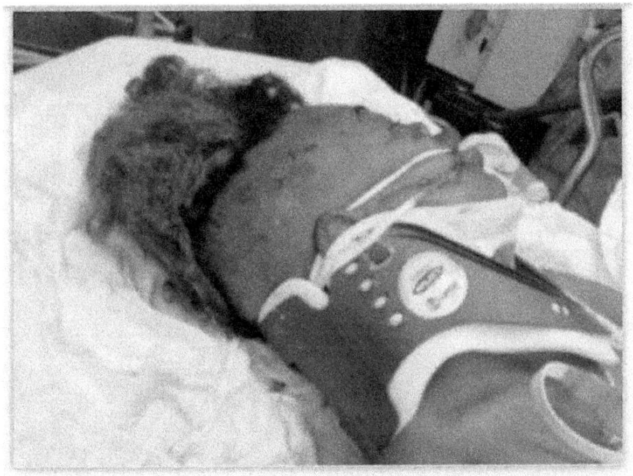

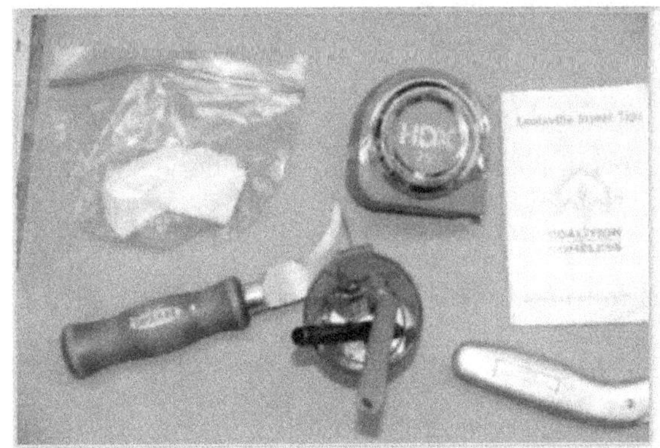

(found at the crime scene)

CHAPTER 9

When I finally wake up months later, the next thing I know is I have been in a coma for 3 months. I was told how I was delirious, pulling out machines and tubes. They learned the only time I would calm down was if a picture of my son was shown to me. I was informed by the detectives that there was another DNA found in my rape kit, but the evidence was only enough to narrow it down but not enough to say conclusively, but I had an idea.

*****

A PHOENIX IS BORN AUG 18,2016

August 18th was the day that I awoke from my 3-month coma. I had no memory of what took place, I was only told stories. But there was this one story that no one could tell me. Honestly, it felt like I had an intervention with Jehovah God, basically showing me that if I continued down the path that I was on, the probability of me living a good life was slim to none. I felt like he showed me where it would leave me if I continued down that path. On the other hand, he also showed me that it's my purpose to be a voice for domestic violence and tap into my talent.

*****

When I first learned from the detectives about what had taken place that day, I was in total disbelief because I had never thought he would take it to this extreme. I learned so much that when they first declared what happened to me, I was in disbelief, thinking that there was no way he could do this to the mother of his child. But once I got time with myself, sitting and meditating on it, the answer did not seem so out of reach. It took me a couple of days to really digest the fact of the matter that he actually tried to take my life. Now, all the vicious attacks that he did on me made me question, "Why." I had no reason or understanding of the reasons behind his actions. That's where I learned the amount of damage that my body endured .....

- 3 month coma
- 2 Brain bleed
- Brain swell
- Stroke
- Rape 1st degree
- Sodomy
- 25-30 broken or fractured bones throughout my body, not including the back.
- Collapsed left lung.
- broken back The L2 and L3 bone in my lower back
- I had to learn how to do everything from A-Z

There's so much more. These are just a few examples of what my body experienced.

I was able to get a copy of my medical records along with a copy of the police report where I learned even more. It was over 2,000 pictures, including the crime scene, the objects that were used, and evidence of everything. I was able to learn so much stuff of what really occurred and the extent of the damage that my body experienced. I was put in an induced coma due to the severity of the damage. Doctors told the detectives that the probability of me surviving was significantly less. I was incubated, and machines kept me alive with the help of "Jehovah God," who was keeping me alive. I may not have been there physically or mentally, but I can honestly say I do believe I had a divine intervention, and from that moment forth, my life has a purpose. For 3 months, I remained in a coma while my body continued to heal and repair itself. My body and face were unrecognizable. I was labeled a Jane doe with no one knowing who or where I was.

CHAPTER 10

For days leading into weeks and eventually into months, my body lies there. I had a lot of prayers going for me; there was so much activity that I was not aware of. (Right here, I am "here-saying" because I was told these stories of the activity. I was not there mentally or physically...) When I came out of my coma fresh, a nurse told me that "every hour or so, they had to come in and flip my body over so I would not develop bed sores. I could not even flip over in bed. And it took me by surprise when I learned that my domestic violence case became newsworthy, but because of the severity of the situation, my name was not mentioned. I was known as Jane Doe. The only people who knew of my status were the police and detectives. My daddy was the one who had to come and identify my body, and the gruesome details that he remembers are even more gruesome to think about. The way that he describes me is as if I looked like an elephant. My face and head were so big and swollen. My dad said I had a tube connected to my head, and that is where fluids were being released and sucked on top of my skull. He said the way my body looked as if he trampled up and down my body with a Timberland logo etched all up and down with my skin color blue, pink, and red. I was in a coma for three months and had a stroke, too. As a result, it left my hands and left side depleted, requiring even more surgeries. The doctors were concerned about keeping me alive so the splints were not put on my hands as an end result.

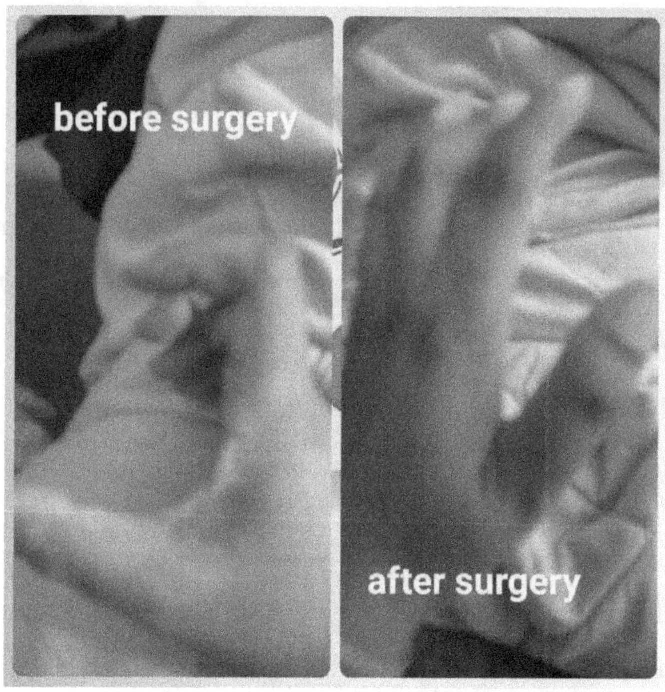

On the left side is my hand before surgery, and on the right hand is where surgery was done. My tendons were cut, and I was not happy with the outcomes, so I decided not to do surgery on the right hand. I have learned to function with the ability to live everyday life. I have handwritten everything in this book before I typed up everything. It's good hand therapy for me!

I spent 3 months in a coma back in my hometown until the police and detectives were worried and concerned about my safety, so

I was moved to another end of the hospital before I was taken out of my state and put where they felt it was a safer distance. When I was put into protective custody, I remained there for 5.6 years, and that meant no communication with family and my son, which was by far the hardest with everything I have been through just watching my son grow up in pictures.

I spent years regaining my strength. I was forced to retrain my mind and my brain from what I had previously learned that I already knew how to do. I had to learn how to breathe, talk, and eat on my own. Learning how to talk was a test. It was very difficult to learn to make simple conversations, to pronounce and raise my voice, to just be heard. Even when it came to the learning to walk aspect, It was a journey. I lived with a tracheostomy for several years before I was finally able to dispose it off and start breathing on my own. I have been successfully able to get rid of every device that was ever given to me to survive and live a life. I spent years learning to walk, talk, and function as an adult again.

CHAPTER 11

I never complained, even though it was extremely hard. There were times I did not know how I was going to make it. My body was so tired and worn out. It felt like I worked a whole shift at work when I was actually not doing anything. I would just lie there in my bed, and my bones hurt so bad that my ache had an ache.

My once long and beautiful hair was now all cut off into a curly afro.

*****

I spent years and months in hiding, and I was only able to look and enjoy life through social media. I was not allowed to have an account, so I created a dummy account where I could live virtually through pictures. As a mother, I had to learn details about my family and the actions that I had been missing. I was only able to learn about my child through phone calls and pictures. That really put a huge strain on the relationship that I was trying to build with him. I saw old friends and family that left me in awe. All the things I have learned are details of what I have been missing over the years. I really felt like I missed a lot of life and moments. My once small cousins were now grown-up family members with their own families. I missed out on so much that I started to feel as if I was like a lost past-tense memory.

Journal entry 01-2-2021

I just got off the phone with my daddy and had a real-life realization of what my son is going through emotionally. When I finally got to put the pieces together and fully understood what my son was going through and feeling, I broke down in tears. Now I'm going to break it down; maybe you'll tear up as well.

1. POINT ONE - My son had been going to counseling and therapy a couple of times a week. With every visit, he always brings up the story about me, his dad, and him that only we know about. Nobody knows this story except us. Well, comes to my understanding at the age of 8, yes, he still remembers it. The story goes as follows: All three of us were in the black Camaro headed to get some ice cream. Our son was buckled up back in his seat, his daddy was in the driver's seat, and I was in the passenger seat. I had gotten a shake, and the lil man got an ice cream in a cup. We decided to go and sit outside under an umbrella table while we waited for Daddy to come back out from picking up our order. He came back, we sat out and ate our ice creams, enjoying the day and our time together. Before long, we decided to go and get out of the hot sun; I still had my milkshake with me as we got into the car after buckling our son back up. We settled in the car while talking to our lil man about how much fun we had with him. Don't know what exactly happened, but the energy quickly changed because I had dropped my cup accidentally, but it didn't leave much of a mess. Either way, he got mad, and the next thing I remember was a SLAP across my face, leaving me stinging in pain!

2. Every time he goes to counseling, he always brings it up.

3. Now, every time I talk with him through video, some calls are good, but then on the other calls, he is very standoffish.

4. Now, I couldn't understand why until I talked with my daddy and realized something.

5. My son asked for his daddy's number, not knowing he was in jail, but he wanted his number so he could tell him that he wanted some new shoes.

6. Now, all he remembers from his daddy is that daddy spoiled him when we were all together.

7. For him to keep bringing that up every time he talks with the workers means that the only memory he has of his parents together is the smack from his daddy to his mommy.

8. All memories about his daddy are good, but one he has with me is that smack across the face.

9. All that being said, he was a toddler then. In his mind, I'm thinking is, 'Mommy got hit by Daddy', and now both Mommy and Daddy are gone.

10. I'm wondering what's in his mind. Maybe he thinks I did something wrong because we were both gone.

11. Now, I'm painted as the bad mother because mommy got hit by daddy, and with no understanding of what has happened and what's still going on.

12. Like I'm trying to regain my emotions together, like as much as I possibly can, because it hurts me right now.

13. He's got mixed emotions about who his mother really is. (On the one hand, Mommy is someone who always buys and sends me gift cards, and pictures and gifts. On the other hand, Daddy hits Mommy, and they are both gone).

14. So, for me, that makes me think that he's mixed with emotions and feelings about what is really going on.

15. Present day - Mommy gone, Daddy gone. Mommy buys me gifts me and talks to me on video phone calls.

16. In the back of my mind, I'm thinking my cousin said he only acts out in school when he talks to me now. 'HIM' didn't realize it had a huge impact not only on me but it caused a huge impact on our child as well. HIM didn't realize what it would do to him and what would be going

through his mind. Now he's got mixed feelings and emotions about what he remembers and what it's going to do to his mental state as well.

I'm like, No! He didn't think that; he was only focused on hurting me! Yes, I may not know about what exactly took place on that fateful date and times when he was destroying my body, but I know in due time, all will be revealed with faith and my personal investigation of what really took place. I do know that all the answers will be revealed! Oh, and not to mention the fact that I have on paper a police report that was made.

Chapter 12

Journal entry-June 29th, 2022-

I'm just sitting here thinking about and feeling good, just enjoying my smoke! So I have been thinking to myself, I know when I had that dream, I felt like it was a dream God envisioned me to have. It's like I was lying down on the floor of what looked like a townhouse, and I was smoking a blunt. I was writing something down, but I didn't know what it was. But I was! So within saying that, I finally was able to get a way to the DMV, so the next Tuesday, I'm going there, and I'm so excited to be a step closer once I get my ID. They said it got to be another waiting game because I heard they mail it to you now to get it and go. But only when I get the ID and it's legit that I can finally sign up for my housing. I'm going for the townhouse; that's what my heart wants. It's a must-have on a patio or a balcony because I would not be smoking in my house. I really want a fitness center there or close by because I'm going to do my own exercising and make sure I keep up with my personal therapy. That's why I really want a fitness center either on that property or in close proximity. Those are a must, but I'm getting ready to enter the world again soon. My only thought is, "Will I be ready"?

**** *****

-Journal entry -8-7-2022-

Today was a good day for me. I got some good news today. For the past 5 years, I have been trying to piece together the story of my past life and what happened to me because I don't remember anything. I have been requesting my medical records from where I used to live. I have been trying to get them records for months, and I finally got it today!

I got my nerves together, and then I started looking at the email. It contained 678 pages of my day at the hospital, and I was reading through it, but there were a couple of things I didn't understand. So, I went out to the nurses' station and asked her what some words meant, and then I went back to my room, and I began reading more and more, and it was all just baffling,

I have on my butt like it looks like a whole bunch of scars that looked like a whole bunch of scars or cut marks. It looked like it was used as a cutting board. This is going somewhere, but no I have always wondered what happened, and today I found out what exactly happened on my butt.

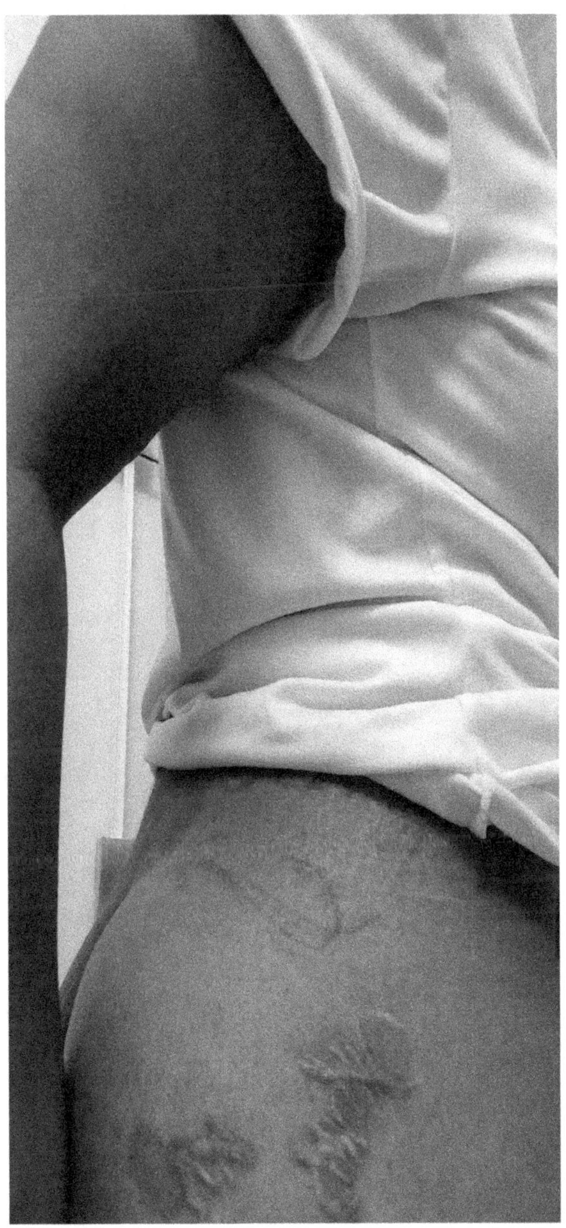

The way that he discarded my body, he basically treated my body like it was trash. The way I look at it is that my scars are now a part of my life story. Every scar I have from this man that he has taken from me, he tried to rewrite my story, but I'm back! All my scars are a story to be told, and I am going to tell this story so maybe I'll send him a copy of my book, and he can read about how he tried to destroy my life, but God had other plans for my life. My police record reads, "The victim appeared to have human bite marks on the inside of her leg and buttocks with a gaping open wound which appears to be human bite impressions." I'm not a genius, but it says, "A human bite mark? So he tried to "bite me." It also says, "The victim had wounds at numerous places that had the same characteristics of an edged instrument insertion." He sodomized me with that edged instrument.

CHAPTER 13
2017

In the nursing home, I was known as "One of God's chosen ones" because no matter the condition I was in, my spirit would not settle. Everybody could sense that there was some type of purpose in my life. There is a reason. I knew I was not to be in that position. I always felt like I was in a shell. I was alive in the shell, but I was living my life through glasses, and I knew that I would not have him have the last say over my life. I knew I was not going to be content living in that position for the rest of my life. I could not at all take care of myself, even down to the simplest things, such as breathing and moving. I vaguely remember that stage of my life. I only know of the stories that I was told by the workers. They said that during the time that my body had to be rotated every other hour, they recalled a story that they remembered. They were walking past my room when they picked their head in to check on me, that I was sitting up. I was in the upright position on my bed, sitting straight up, and that took everyone by surprise. That's when it was noticed "that my spirit was not content with the surrendering mode and to give in. It was my spirit telling me that this was not my final stop and that there was more in me to reach the level I knew I could achieve. This was just to see where my faith and my trust were, how strong it was. I believe that everything that I have experienced is to be a part of my testimony.

I can remember one night when I was fresh in my recovery and one night in the middle of the night, and I don't know if it was a dream that I had in my mind or what, but I had the urge to go to the restroom. I was wearing briefs, but in my mind, I was up and walked to the bathroom. I remember I got up from my bed and took a couple of steps before I fell and hit the floor!

CHAPTER 14

I had developed a serious post-traumatic stress disorder diagnosis because I just never felt comfortable being around people, especially men. I never left my room; I had a private room, and I never wanted to be around men, groups, or crowds of people. I developed a serious trust issue, so I stayed with myself but remained cordial at the same time. For years, I followed the rules there, but the more I became a newer version of myself, the more I started to regain a sense of self again. As I was recovering, I had gotten strong enough that when I saw an elderly person struggling, it was always in my nature to help someone. I know firsthand what it felt like not being able to do something, so I would always extend a hand, and it used to grind certain worker's gear!

I constantly wanted to remain in therapy. I was determined to get my body back in good physical condition. It was not easy; I spent years learning.

I was able to grow a real friendship with two girls who were the same age as me. There were only three young people in the nursing home, and that included me and the two sisters. We were together for over eight years. We traveled to two different nursing homes, and with the move, I really grew a close bond with the sisters Emily and Sydney, and to this very day, I make sure that I keep in very close contact with my sister. Unfortunately, because they were sick, the younger sister passed away on Jan 1, 2021. I felt as if I lost a loved one, but in return, that only drew a closer bond between me and Emily. I'm very well connected to her because I told her she has a sister for life in me. She was with me for eight years in the nursing home. Both sisters suffer from a life-threatening disease, which is HUNTINGTON's DIS-EASE, and it's a terminal illness. I hated to see someone that I grew so close with to be dealing with this disease, and she knows it. During my eight years in the nursing home, she was always one constant. Traveling to two nursing homes, our bond only grew closer, and even though we were in different stages of our lives, I still am a constant in her life. I still keep in touch with the family, and I go visit her often!

****

I was an "Okay" resident. I spoke up for myself and unfair things, especially when it came to my girl Emily. Oh, they hated that because they knew of the close bond I shared with the family, and I was very aware of things, so I would say something if I felt my girl was mishandled or treated because she could not speak for herself clearly enough to where she could be understood. They hated the way I always looked out for her; sorry but not sorry, it's in my nature. I remained to myself, but I also was very aware of my situation, and once I got the memory back enough to function on my own, I became more of a new self. It had got to the point where my bond with Emily was becoming unbreakable. I have a close relationship with her side of the family. I remember we shared this joke that we were indeed related because her stepfather was African American, so that was the joke, he was my father, and her mother was my stepmother. I developed a really close relationship with her whole team to a point I can't remember. We had a celebration of her life, and we went to Newport Aquarium, which was a very magical experience. I'm just blessed and thrilled that they were considerable enough to ask me to come along because they also know the work and the love that I have for Emily.

Nov 27, 2022

CHAPTER 15

Little by little, I slowly started shedding all the tools and machines that were needed to keep me alive. One by one, they all disappeared, but not without a lot of work. I had to learn the basics of learning to breathe on my own. For a long time, I was too small, so I had to pick up weight, and the tube feed was not enough. I had to learn to eat, starting with liquid form, then mechanical, and then regular. I have had to learn to walk again. My left side of my body and my legs were contracted, resulting from the 3 month coma and stroke that affected my left side. Learning how to walk is a daily job, and I only wish I had pictures to show, but I had to learn step by step to walk. To this very day, I am still using a walker as a device to balance out my walking pattern. It took a couple of years for me to learn how to walk. I remember I loved therapy because I knew in my heart that I wanted to do better for myself, so I enjoyed going to therapy, and even when I had no therapy, I tried to still do my therapy in my room. It took me a couple of years to learn how to do the smallest to walking, and it started from me learning how to sit myself up in the bed.

Unfortunately, I do not have an exact timeline as far as the exact dates, but this is still the timeline of the story of my life.

I was not sure of the love I was receiving from the nursing home. I did not know if their love and attention came from caring or just their job, but I grew a lot of love and attention around the nursing home when it came to staff. I had gotten close with a couple of staff members, and in their private time, they always took the extra effort to make sure I was okay. I had an aide, and she always made sure my grooming was up to date. She always takes care of my hair and my eyebrows! I had another aide who also took the extra effort in his downtime. He would walk me through the hallways so I could get strong enough to walk again, and he always made sure I was well-fed. When I started out, I was less than a hundred pounds, and no matter how much I ate, I was not gaining a substantial amount of weight. I gained enough weight to be tested and finally taken off of the tube feed, and when that happened, my friend and the aide made a bet with me. He bet he could make me gain weight. I took on that challenge, and I now call myself Deborah because I was always fed food that will make you gain weight, such as Little Debbie snacks! Little Debbie made me Deborah!

CHAPTER 16

For years, I remained in secrecy and in hiding. And there I was, watching and hearing my son being raised. " I can honestly say," I have never cried over my personal problems, but I can honestly say the only time that I have cried is when it came to my child and his feelings. I also cried, when I found out Mr had passed away. We had just gotten back in contact with each other, so that was a very hard blow. Upon learning of his passing, I was very hurt, to say the least. We've made so many plans on reconnecting, but on a whole nother level than where we left things off years ago. I was elevated in so many ways. I was looking forward to reconnecting with him, but his name for me will always live on, and that's on 1huned!

*****

Time after time, I physically began to get stronger. It was not at all an easy process. I started out from the basics, just learning how to physically sit up on my own. Having to be checked and changed was very uncomfortable, knowing that mentally I was trapped, but I knew physically something could be done. Neither my spirit nor my body was content to have to be cared for. All of my nursing home time, I was in protective custody, so I was never caught in any pictures. I really had good moments that should have been caught on film, such as when I was learning how to walk again. It will be a blessing when I conquer all the tasks, and I look forward to doing more. I was 25 when I was first admitted into the nursing home. I remained in protective custody for 5.6 years. I mentally and physically had to learn how to do what I already previously knew how to do. I had the chance to reinvent myself, even if that meant having to relearn everything so that I could become and feel a 2.0 version of myself.

****

My first pair of walking shoes! These are the shoes that were given to me by the police force involving my case. They brought me these shoes because I honestly had to start over from nothing. "My situation humbled me in so many ways because I went from having everything that money could buy to having nothing. It's a very humbling situation and has made me a very humble person. Everything that I have now I am very grateful, and I value everything in my possession.

CHAPTER 17
2021

For 5.6 years, I was in protective custody, and I remained there until August 2021, when he was finally captured. After almost two years, the war was finally coming to an end.

From the moment I was no longer in hiding, I wanted nothing more than to reach out to my son and family. I was ready to get my identity back, starting with my name! Over the next couple of months, I did everything I had to get my identification back. I may not have had the squeaky clean identity, but it was my identity. It identified who I was.

⚜⚜⚜⚜

Once I had finally gotten all my legal documents to confirm my identity, even though I was anxious to relive my life on another wisdom filled with more educated knowledge on life, over the waiting period, I was in the process of rebuilding and rejuvenating my mind, life, and body. It was almost a decade, 8.5 years, to be exact. I was very determined not to let HIM have the last say over my life. Over the last 5+ years, I was mentally and physically preparing for my return into the world, even though I was now re-entering the world with some "differences" in my body. I will not call them disabilities. I was going into a world with a brand new person, both physically and mentally level. Before this event took place, the type of girl I was, was a girl who lived on the edge, but now, after this life-changing situation, I believe I am a different woman both spiritually and mentally. I personally see what Jehovah God can do. I have experienced it. I felt like I had a one-on-one with him. He showed me where my life was headed, and he gave me a chance and opportunity to change and follow the purpose that he has made for my life .****

The relationship with my son is "a work in progress." I feel he is still very young to know what has taken place. I will not put that on his heart at such a young age, but as the Lord is my witness, my son will know the complete truth. I want him to really know and understand that I did not voluntarily leave on my own accord. I want him to know the truth. I will never hide or lie to my child. I want a tight bond and relationship with my son and the distance and misunderstanding that he has to grow up with. I really want for us to have an understanding and grow our personal bond.

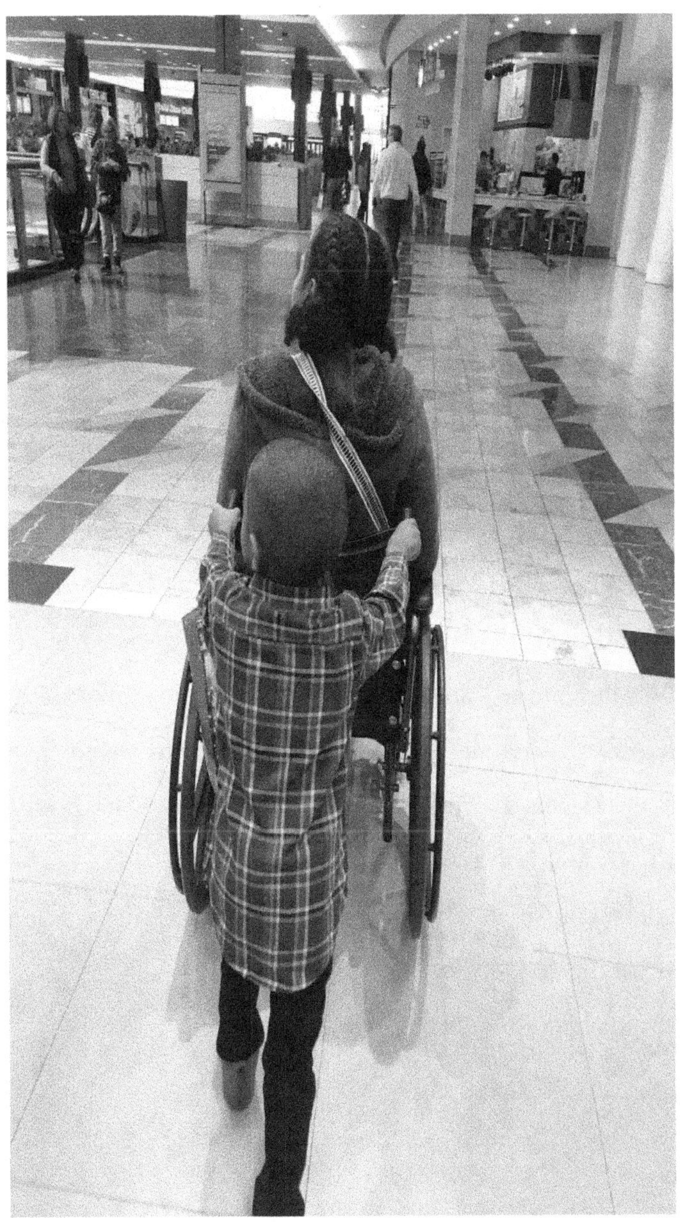

(First visit) "2022" My first time to visit with my son after five years of being in protective custody. We met up at a mall. "The first time I remember seeing him, I honestly didn't know how to react.

Like, I didn't want to be too much and scare him away, but I didn't want him to think or feel I was not interested in seeing him. It has been over a 5 year period since I was last present in his life. We exchanged gifts, and once the nerves were gone, the smiles and hugs came! It's a relationship, and I will always water and grow.

I truly believe in my heart that once my son gets older, and start to question stuff and look for answers. I'm going to let him know the doors are open for whenever he's ready to talk. There is no relationship I value and want more than a relationship and bond with him. He's been misled in so many ways, and I feel like I'm the only one who could fix things and answer the questions he may have. I always tell myself that when that day comes, I'm going to be as honest as he needs. I want him to know that I may have made a silly decision years ago that left a trickling effect, but I have been trying to right my wrongs ever since, and even though the road HAS not been easy, it's a road I will always travel no matter the turbulence. He has taken everything from me, but I always had one thing, and that was God and a growing faith.

****

CHAPTER 18

I got my nerves together, and then I started looking at the email and it contained 678 pages of my days at the hospital and I was reading through it and there was a couple things I didn't understand, so I went out to the nurses station and I asked the nurse what some words meant and after she told me I went back to my room and I began reading more and more and it was just baffling,

8-23-2022

I have been really dragging my feet as far as I'm really taking the time to go through the pictures of that deadly night. But now I really have the time and gumption to start going through these pictures. I have looked at a couple of them, just like pictures of the scene, and I have actually learned that the fight actually happened at the house that we shared together. That right there was a shock to me because I thought where my body was found was where it actually happened. This man sounds like after he beat me to a bloody pulp where my body lay lifeless. I guess he thought I was dead, so he carried me out to the car and drove me to where he threw my body out like trash. Omg, I cannot believe I think I may have figured out the reason. I'm not sure of it, but it makes sense to me now! I'm really going to continue to go through the whole thing. And I'm thinking maybe I could put the puzzles together and figure out what exactly happened. I know a lot of people did not understand why I wanted to know what happened. The only reason that I want to know what happened is because I look at it like this. I cannot start a new book in my life if I have not finished the other one, like, I want to end it knowing why I'm "Beautify Different". For the rest of my life, I have to live with the fact that my life and my physical body are forever changed for the remainder of my life. I honestly believe It's now time for me to finally pull the band-aid completely off. In the end, I know the only ones who really know what actually happened are him and God.

Even though this is my reality now, I'm still coming to terms with the reality of it. I have to rely on a medical device of some sort to properly keep walking and balancing myself. I have to understand that I aim to be the victor. I will not allow my new shortcomings to become who I am. I am much more than that, and that's something I realized through the grace of God, by him allowing me a second chance at life to do things better and to live out my purpose, whatever that might actually be.

This shirt my family got done in support during the court dates.

My Sister
Is My
Hero
Fight
Domestic
Violence

CHAPTER 19

On 9-15-2022, the case was finally over. After five years, it was finally over. It was a long overdue case that did not give the results that were needed, and I was not happy, nor was I surprised by the outcome. After all that time and the journey I traveled, I felt like I was not justified. My family attended every court date, and when the judge read off that He decided to take a plea deal, my family lost it. I can remember I was on the conference call when the judge was done reading his sentence. The response I heard was, "13 years, what the f**k. My family was in an uproar. He was basically pleading the fifth, not owning up to anything, keeping a tight lip. I thank God for DNA. Everyone was in an uproar and in bewilderment because we could not understand how a person could get all these serious charges like attempted murder and other big charges (I'm not going to air out the details on that), but I learned after the fact of the details of what took place during the court proceeding during and after it was over. During one court proceeding, it was said that HIM had a smart smirk on his face. After my dad caught a glimpse of his facial expression, anger instantly filled up, and without thinking, my dad lunged over the banister and separator. He was headed in HIM'S direction before my dad was subdued and tackled by the guards. I was happy to learn about my family having my back! I was never discouraged. I may have been disappointed, but I was never discouraged because I always said, "God is my vindicator. I know that "He is righteous, just, and fair. I don't look to men for answers. He has to face the main judge in the sky, so I don't put my faith in man. I spent years rebuilding myself, and not only was I affected, but our families were also affected. They had to also go through the emotional journey of not knowing if I would survive to see the next day. I have nothing against our legal system, for it brought my abuser to the front, but I know Jehovah God is going to be the one who gives the appropriate and final verdict. I also learned that after a court proceeding, one of his associates made a smart remark that my family overheard. "He should have killed her" is what was said before all hell broke loose. My sisters overheard the comment, and that's all it took before hits were licked upon her face and her cell phone was destroyed, and rightly so. She had no nerves to say that when she was in the wrong. I was glad to learn that my family had my back because that girl deserved it. I remember she was the same girl, and I suspected something weird was going on with them. I recall one time HIM had just had a little field day on my body in the house, and then after he was done, he called this girl over to the house. "They had unknown plans." when she came into the house, she just looked at me and continued on with him, leaving me there looking and feeling stupid and embarrassed. She turned a blind eye to what she saw and continued a sneaky relationship with HIM. I never found the reason for this, and even though I have gone to every avenue to find the answer to my question, I'm coming to terms with the fact that I may never know the reason why he viciously attacked me. I know HIM and God may be the only ones who know the reason, but I know when the day and time comes, he is going to have to answer him for his reasoning, and God will handle the judgment.

Even though he decided on taking a deal, I was not able to face him in court because of the COVID restrictions. I was looking forward to facing him. I wanted to face him and see his facial expression when he saw what God had restored from what he had tried to destroy. I was disappointed that I could not face him, but I was able to read him my victim impact statement over a conference call. In the court at full attention, I read :

9-15-2022

-My Victim Impact Statement –

"I have not lived a perfect life, and I have paid for the choices I have made. In 2016, after being incarcerated and away from my home for over all these years, all I wanted was to work on staying on the right path. Most of all, I wanted to be reunited with my son, with our son. There is nothing more that I wanted than to be a proper mother. I wanted to break the cycle of abuse and being in the system. I did not want our son to be another statistic. The opportunity to live the life that I had envisioned for my son and myself was taken from me. This is not me, but when I look in the mirror, I see the shell I live in now. He left me for dead, caused me to have a stroke, left me in a coma for three months, caused me to have multiple surgeries, and caused two brain injuries. Tubes and machines are what kept me alive like a newborn baby. I had to learn to breathe on my own, talk, walk, even turn over in bed. I was a woman who was forced into infancy. Now, due to my brain injury, I have no sense of smell, and I cannot taste, and that's not even a piece of the damage you caused. As a result of his actions, I suffer from Post-Traumatic-Syndrome-Disorder, and I do not trust people. I am very uneasy around anyone of the opposite sex. I suffer from night terrors and will have to always be on medications to help me manage the anxiety that I feel on a daily basis. Our son is hurting. He was forced into a life that I did not want for him. He is growing up without a mother or a father, for I am thankful he has a good home, but he will have to grow up with finding out what his father did to his mother. I am disappointed that my questions about why this was done may be left unanswered. The impact of this has physically and mentally changed me forever. I choose to no longer carry the burden of anger that I once felt for you instead, I will leave my forgiveness for you at the cross!

--End

I spent months after the final sentencing trying to get my affairs back in order.

Mar 27-2023- Official discharge from nursing home

****

CHAPTER 20

As for me, my life has just begun. I'm walking out into the world with a whole new mindset, even though I may be walking out with an extra device to keep me up straight and balanced. I have a whole new goal. After almost 8.5 years, I could finally and officially learn to live the new life I have been given a second chance. After all those years, our child, who knows firsthand, unfortunately, is a victim of our circumstances and poor choices. I can't go back and right my wrongs, but I can do things differently. I now have a chance to make better decisions in life and to prioritize better in life with my personal life.

Mar 27,2023-

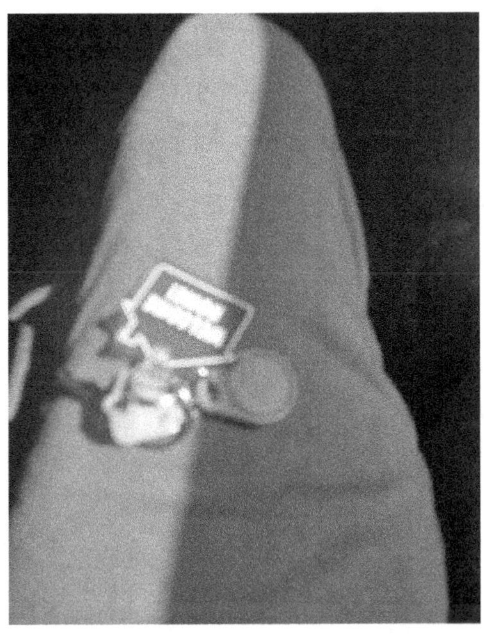

For I know there is a purpose for my life just to see firsthand all the work that he has done in my life. I will never take for granted any moment of this second chance that I have been given to make something out of my life to live my purpose, and I hope my message really shows through this book. I want to show that I'm living proof of obstacles after obstacles, that no matter the difficulties life may throw your way, you do not give up. There have been many trials and obstacles in life that may be or get in your path, and even if you stumble or get off the path, you do not give up or give in. There have been many times throughout my life that I honestly felt defeated, and at times, I felt it would be easier and a relief if I just gave up or allowed any of my circumstances to hold me back and swallow me whole. I have experienced it firsthand, having to learn all the basic things in life all over again. I had to relearn how to live. So, with that being said, I have survived this no matter what man may throw my way. I know that with God and the strength he gave me, I can conquer anything!

I'm walking out into the world again as a new and redefined person with a whole new mindset. Will I be able to conquer this new journey of life now? Will I be able to get my relationship back on track with my son? Will I allow my physical limitations to limit me? There are so many unanswered questions, but I'm not afraid to tackle these new life obstacles. I know I can and will overcome them. I know if I gave up throughout this whole process, I realize that whatever Jehovah God has for me, I would have never seen if I gave up because it was hard or difficult. I have not seen quite what my purpose is exactly, but I am following my spirit in my heart. I know better things are awaiting me. I look at life in a whole new way, and I know that I shouldn't live or view life in the way that I do, but it works for me; it gets me through my day-to-day. I know as I go through my daily life, things will get second nature, but as of right now, I'm taking it one step at a time to unveil how I will conquer this mountain. I let the love I had for him blind me so much that my all was given. I lost myself, and now my blinders have been removed. It's time to run and enjoy the race called life.

- End-

A message to the reader

As I'm sitting back, I'm thinking to myself about the journey I have been on and how good God has been in my life. I'm always in amazement, seeing him work through my life, like when I was basically pronounced dead, but God saw that, and he brought me back. I had enough life left in me, and with my God's help, I was reborn. As my body was rebuilding itself, I had to learn to live my life over again from a baby, and growing up, I went as far as having someone change me to change my briefs and care for me or flip me over in the bed so I wouldn't get bed sores. I have made progress along the way. To be able to function like a human, learn how to breathe on my own without living on machines to keep me alive. To learn how to even eat, I went from the baby stage to adulthood, so now I can eat some food for real, LOL! With all that said, learning how to walk again like a toddler taking their first steps, I went through the whole stages, and I'm currently walking with a walker. I can also walk by myself, but I can only go so far before I get tired or my legs get weak and I can't take it. Yes, I may be left with a few physical disabilities, but ain't nothing that I cannot overcome.

So, I had two dreams on two separate nights. Both have the same topic, but I saw them on different nights, and that's why I feel like it was God speaking to me....

Night 1, in this particular dream, HIM was in prison, and he was in the day room, looking up at the TV and watching something with his arms over his head. A commercial came on, and it was an ad of me promoting my book. I even remember the position I was in on my book that was one dream.

Night 2, in this dream, HIM once again was in the day room, but this time he was sitting at a table flipping through some magazines on the table. As he flips through the magazines, he runs across another ad of me promoting my book. I still was in the same position in the book. Everything was good. So, I took that like there was nothing but a message from God!

Night? This dream took place around my birthday. I was lying on the floor of my townhouse, writing something and smoking a blizzy! Then fast forward to today, which is July 22nd. I had received an email from our social worker, and she was letting me know. She said to meet me in the office at 8:30, so I went to her office, but she wasn't there. A door was closed, and I walked to the receptionist desk where my favorite worker, who's been with me as the D.O.N of this establishment. I showed her the email that I received. That's when she informed me that the people from the Home Choice Program were on their way to talk to me. Now, Home Choice is an establishment where they partner with Section 8 and help with housing. So it's just something like it's just two days away from my birthday, and I received some of the best news like they're looking for my housing, and they're getting me set up to return to the world.

Like, oh no, if you really open your ears and understand God is communicating with you, you have to be quiet and listen and talk with him! I'm still trying to understand my project fully, but until then, I will continue to work on and travel the road that's been paved for me.

I bravely decided to tell the truths of my life because I felt it was a part of my purpose to tell my story and what I have been through. There were times I thought about ending it like I was physically, mentally, and emotionally tired. I was drained on all levels; it did seem easier to just give up. I did not want to keep going. To me, it all seemed pointless to me. As many times I tried to quit life, there was always a voice in my head that would talk me off the ledge and have me retreat back into reality and face the facts that I was scared and that I didn't really want to hurt myself and I was allowing the pain and emotional hurt to consume me and the pain had become my identity.

Also, I really want to say something about an area that I feel needs more light on, and that is domestic violence. I experienced years of abuse not only physically but emotionally as well. With every fight, it made me feel less of a woman, less of a human being. I would feel so helpless, but all at the same time, I loved him, and I began to tell myself. If he didn't love me, he wouldn't go so hard on me. It was a way he was just expressing his love and emotions. It took him almost permanently ending my life for me to realize he didn't give a damn about me for him to allow me to suffer in the way he did. It just shows the amount of love and respect he had for me. It took me experiencing near death at his hands for me to finally understand that that was not love. That was pure hatred. I learned for the couple of months that I was with him when nobody knew of my whereabouts or my existence. For months, I was with him, and this was the outcome of my being with him. For a couple of months, I had no recollection or memory of what really happened and what made him lose it like he did. I have spent years trying to put the pieces together to understand how and why it unfolded. I have gotten my police report and hospital reports, and it required so many pictures of the scene and of my body. I did not know a lot of the things I learned, and so with that, I wanted to look further into why. No matter how far I looked, I was not able to come up with anything. So, for now, it remains a mystery, but like in the game clue, soon the answers would be revealed, and that chapter of my life would finally have a period at the end rather than a coma.

I have also learned that your body and your brain ultimately block out very traumatic events in your life, and even though I want to know the reasons behind the attack, I may never find out, and I have to be okay with that. I may be living a very different life now, but I have to look at that as a blessing in itself because I have the chance to do things differently and make better decisions. I now know and value what's important in my life and who I need to put first in my life, and that is my child. He deserves to know the truth because he has not been given a life that I never envisioned for him, and even though he is still young, I know firsthand that memories and unknown feelings surface back up and never stay buried forever.

I'm not claiming our whole relationship was all violent. We've had some very good and laughable moments, but always looming in the shadows was terror waiting to be unleashed. Always following after every falling out, all was forgiven after a couple of sweet gestures and saying the words that made my guard come all the way down. I was weak for him. I was in love with him, but after this ordeal, I had to learn how to love myself first. I know if I had loved myself first, I would have never subjected myself to that kind of abuse and torture. I know through all of the struggles, at least the good thing was to come out of it, and that is my son. You lost your privilege, but through this ordeal, I was ultimately able to find myself and who I am, and it turns out I love the person I am, and who I am becoming, and where I am headed. That's UP! I was so used to the hurt that I became afraid and cautious of anything or anyone. I always had a fear of being hurt again, so I have learned to put up a wall not to keep people out but to protect myself.

No matter how bad or how hard times may get, I will have faith in what's right in the power of my mind and in God. I will work hard, and success will come in due time. These are my wings, and with those, I will rise like the Phoenix that I am!

I really hope you enjoyed hearing my story.

Thank you!

The playlist that kept me going and strong

- ✓ Still Standing- Monica
- ✓ You should have killed me- K. Michelle ft Rick Ross
- ✓ I'm going to be ready-Yolanda Adams
- ✓ Me-Tamia
- ✓ He still loves me -The fighting Temptations
- ✓ Won't he do it-Koryn Hawthorne
- ✓ Can't give up now-Mary Mary
- ✓ Never would have made it - Marvin Sapp

✓ Love is blind Eve

~Pointers~

One hit > apology > 2nd hit = constant cycle
Some people are afraid to tell their stories with the fear that no one will believe them. They feel ashamed or embarrassed. They make you feel guilty and responsible. They try to make a reason to justify their behavior

They hit you, then they try to apologize, but it happens again. Then you realize that "apology" was just to reel you in a psychological, mental, and emotional trap disguised by "love."

They will make you feel like you need them

*You can Freeze and Appease

Or

You can Fight or Flight*

Domestic Violence Facts

On average, nearly 20 people per minute are physically and intimately abused by their partner in the US, according to the National Coalition Against Domestic Violence.

Domestic victimization is correlated with higher rates of depression and suicidal Behavior.

48.4% of women and **48.8%** of men have experienced at least one psychologically aggressive behavior by an intimate partner.

1 in 4 women and 1 in 7 men have been victims of severe physical violence (e.g., beating, burning, strangling) by an intimate partner in their lifetime.

www.ingramcontent.com/pod-product-compliance
Lightning Source LLC
Chambersburg PA
CBHW052055150726
48002CB00002B/895